Marybeth Romeo

We Should Be So Lucky

Vanguard Press

VANGUARD PAPERBACK

© Copyright 2025
Marybeth Romeo

The right of Marybeth Romeo to be identified as author of this work has been asserted by her in accordance with the Copyright, Designs and Patents Act 1988.

All Rights Reserved

No reproduction, copy or transmission of this publication may be made without written permission.
No paragraph of this publication may be reproduced, copied or transmitted save with the written permission of the publisher, or in accordance with the provisions of the Copyright Act 1956 (as amended).

Any person who commits any unauthorised act in relation to this publication may be liable to criminal prosecution and civil claims for damages.

A CIP catalogue record for this title is available from the British Library.

ISBN 978 1 838794 518 4

This is a work of fiction. Names, characters, businesses, places, events and incidents are either the products of the author's imagination or used in a fictitious manner. Any resemblance to actual persons, living or dead, or actual events is purely coincidental.

Vanguard Press is an imprint of
Pegasus Elliot Mackenzie Publishers Ltd.
www.pegasuspublishers.com

First Published in 2025

Vanguard Press
Sheraton House Castle Park
Cambridge England

Printed & Bound in Great Britain

Dedication

For Ben--my wolf. For Eddie--my healer. For Jonah, Luca, Luna, Piolet, Simba--my dear friends.

We are lucky, you and I.

No really! I mean it. It's true!

When all else fails

which it happens to do...

You're lucky to have me

and I'm lucky to have you.

We are lucky that we found eachother

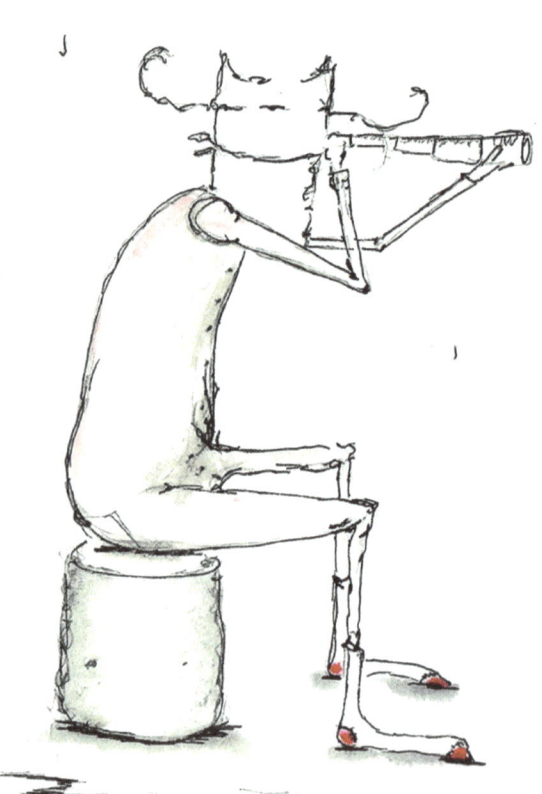

when you think of all the folks out there...

and all the empty space in between.

I mean...

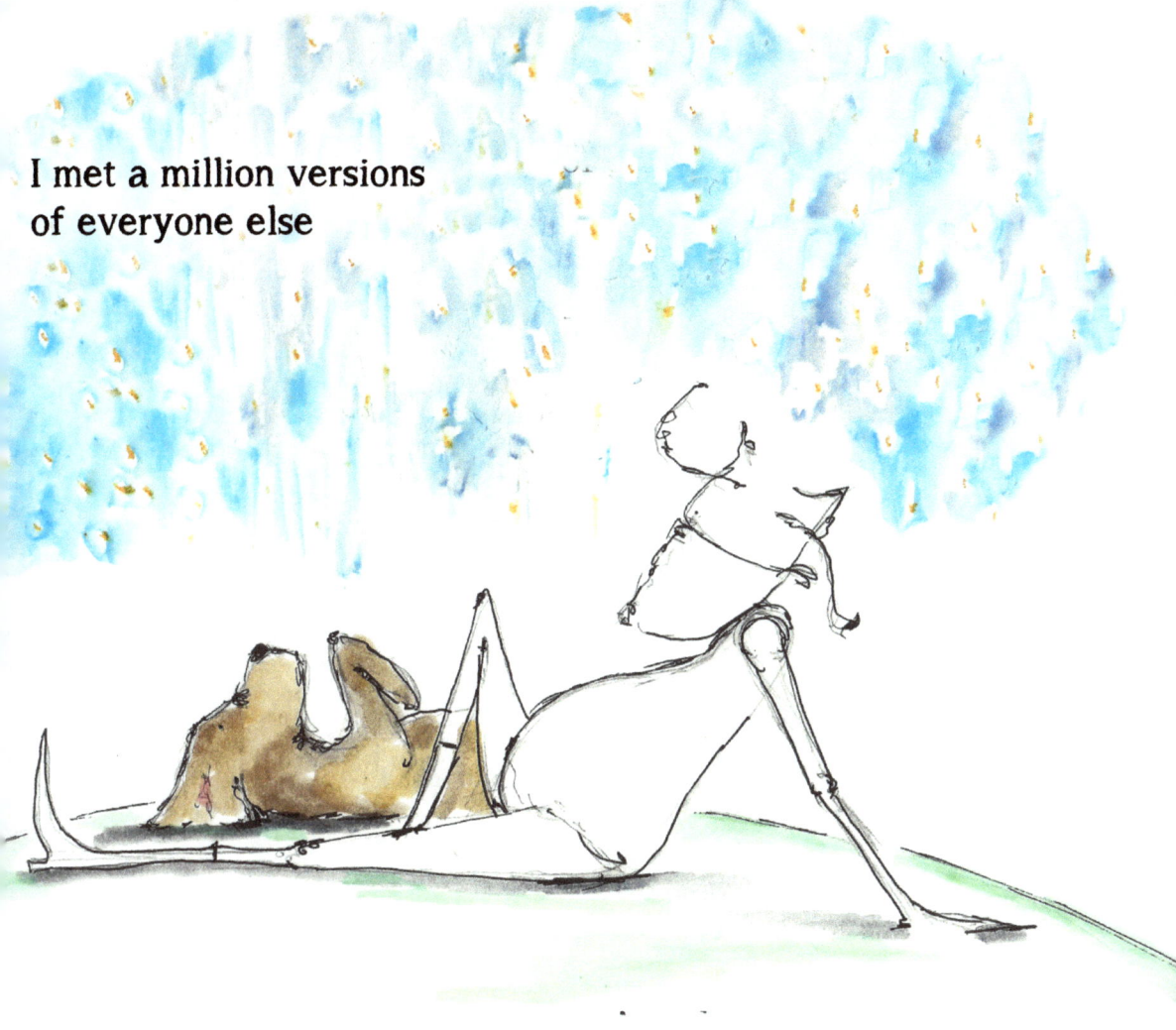

I met a million versions of everyone else

but I'm pretty sure there's only one you.

I know what you're thinking.

That maybe we don't seem,
                    at this particular moment...

or that parlicular moment,

particularly lucky.

But in the sense that I have
you and you have me,

we are lucky
even when we are
not so lucky.

Even if we are not so lucky most of the time.

Like when it rains and we are cooped in (if we're lucky).

Or when it rains and we are shut out (much more likely).

We don't mind being stranded together.

You'll say
aren't we lucky for this unfortunate weather?

Still, sometimes we fall apart.

We're only human after all.

Scratch that!
You're a friggen animal at the friggen zoo!

I never met someone as stubborn as me

until I met someone
as stubborn as you.

Sometimes I can't stand your guts.

But I still want you close.

And sometimes the sight of me makes you sick.

But if you call time out then
I'll call the huddle. *Cuddle?*

I'm safe with you...

that's how I know I am lucky.

You won't up and leave *poof* just like that.

Cause you're not afraid of my gloom.
And a good thing too!

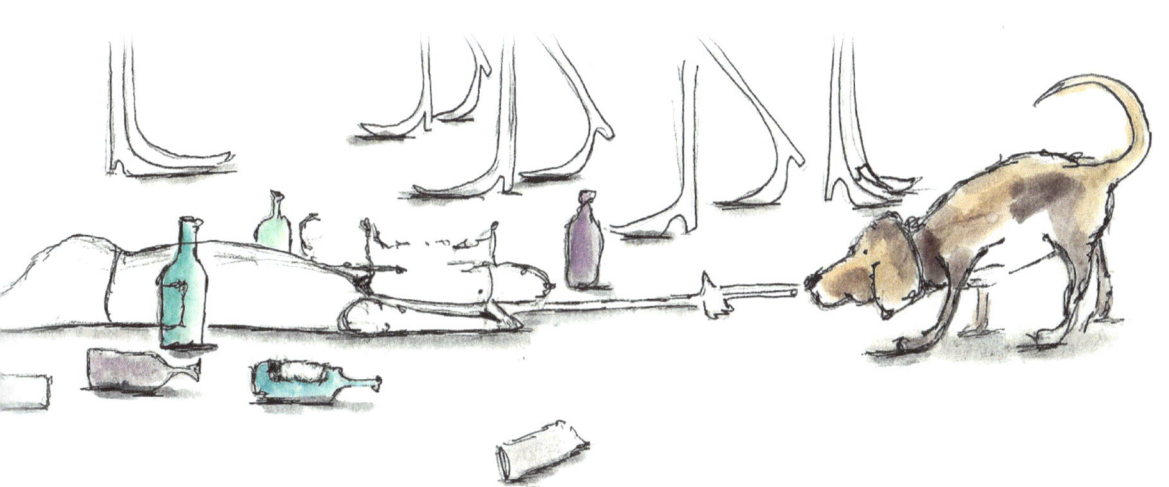

When my heart is heavy
you're the only one I want around.

You'll say
take your time...

but you're not allowed to go far away.

Cause we're a team.

And what happens to me if you give up?

So I've got your back
and you've got mine.

If someone bugs you, then they bug me too.
I don't even need to know why.

And I'm not even faking.
I could scream just thinking about it.

I'd like to march right up and say
hey pal, you feeling lucky?

But don't worry. I won't.

However, if I happen to...

Or I get myself into trouble like I sometimes do...

or if I act a fool

and I embarrass you too...

I know you will like me still.

And I will always like you!

Sometimes so much, I want
to squeeze your friggen head off.

Fact is, you're the greatest.
At least I think so.

And it makes me crazy
when other folks don't know.

They just don't know
how good it could be

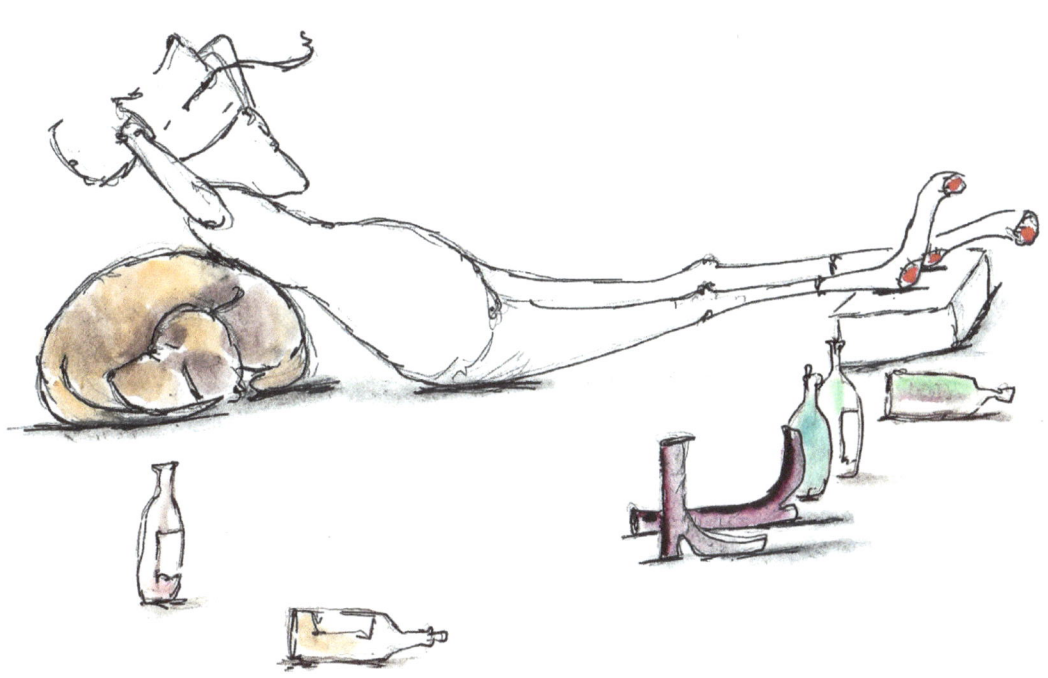

that someone like you
could have someone like me.

And vice versa.
Obviously.

I'll say
folks don't like the looks of us,

and you'll say
that's probably true.

But we'll always belong somewhere.

If you're an outcast with me then I'm an outcast with you.

No really! I mean it. It's true!

We are lucky our fates
are hopelessly bound.

Because your favorite is me

and my favorite is you.

About the Author

Mary Beth Romeo is an accomplished holistic chef and business owner originally from Long Island, NY. She holds a double bachelor's degree in Women's Studies and Writing from Simmons College, and a master's degree in urban Affairs from Hunter College. After ten years of community organizing work, Mary Beth pursued her passion as a healing chef. Alongside her culinary pursuits, she also shares her talent as an illustrator and author. currently residing in beacon New York with her family, Marybeth is the owner/chef of the Meal Collective.

Acknowledgements

...Hang on the walls....

We Should Be So Lucky is not really the story of ONE dog and ONE cowboy, but an anthology of twenty years of friendship and love, and many dogs and many cowboys. As such, I would like to acknowledge the various souls (human and otherwise) whose companionship has contributed to my deeper understanding of relationships—without the complexities between us over the years, nothing about love and like and fortune would make any sense to me. I would like to acknowledge the people who supported cowboy and dog when they debuted as art and greeting cards. Somewhere in the world, 30 originals and 70 prints decorate the homes of people I never met, or never got to know.

I would like to give a special acknowledgement to my dad, who put cowboy and dog in hand made wooden frames when we lived -for a time- as artists; when we braved wind storms and weather, as we sold our collaborations at Brooklyn flea. A small acknowledgement to the fingers he cut off when he made that very last frame. And of course, I would like to acknowledge my mother (you'd like this one, Bets), my sibs and family who rally to my every wild idea; Margaret – the mother of my son, and Ramsey who keeps my life inspired.

www.ingramcontent.com/pod-product-compliance
Lightning Source LLC
Chambersburg PA
CBHW050739110526
44590CB00002B/27